L egend has it that Ernest Hemingway was challenged by some friends to write a story in six words. Hemingway responded to the challenge with the following story: *For sale: baby shoes, never worn.*

The story tickles the imagination. Why were the shoes never worn? Were they too small? Did the baby die? Was the baby not able to wear shoes? Any of these are plausible explanations left up to the reader's imagination.

This style of writing has a number of aliases: postcard fiction, flash fiction, micro fiction, and sudden fiction. Lonnie Pacelli, the series creator, was introduced to this style of writing by a friend over a cup of coffee. He was entranced with the idea and started thinking about how this extreme brevity of writing could apply in today's micro-burst communication culture of text messages, tweets, and wall posts. Thus the inspiration for **Six-Word Lessons**.

In **Six-Word Lessons** you will find 100 short, practical tips and ideas to help with your beauty routines from head to toe. Rather than pore through pages and pages of content trying to search for what you need, **Six-Word Lessons** gives them to you quickly and easily.

My hope is that you're able to use the ideas from **Six-Word Lessons** to improve how you look and feel about yourself day-in and day-out. Tell me how it's impacted you at story@6wordlessons.com.

3

Table of Contents

Get to Know your Body Shape

1

Learn to dress your body type.

There are various names and categories for body types, named after anything from geometric shapes to fruit.

The goal is to know which body areas are larger or smaller and wear clothing styles that make your entire body look more balanced.

2

Don't make large body areas larger.

Obviously, you don't want your largest area to appear even larger because of your clothing, but women do exactly that without realizing it.

For example, shoulder pads with a wide lapel make a large chest and shoulders even larger, and pants with cargo pockets on the thighs will make them look larger.

3

It is O.K. to enlarge something.

Often women have body areas that are too small in proportion to others, such as very small shoulders or hips. Full skirts or cargo pockets can make small hips and thighs appear larger, and wide collars, lapels, puffy sleeves, and shoulder pads can make small shoulders appear larger.

4

Black is not always that slimming.

Wearing black is much too common, and something I would love to see less of. Black can be slimming, but no more so than brown, navy or burgundy. Fit and quality are more important than color.

Black does not flatter everyone's skin tone, and is harsh on many women, so consider some alternative dark neutrals combined with brighter colors.

5

Clothing can improve any woman's shape.

If you take the time and effort to learn about your body type and which clothing best balances out your shape and flatters you, you will look more like your ideal shape, which leads to confidence and success in your chosen career and lifestyle.

Tips for your Terrific Top Half

6

V-necks lengthen your neck and chest.

Wearing a deep V-neck opens up the chest area and gives a nice line up to the neck and throat, flattering the bustline, whether it's large or small.

You can find V-neck garments with or without collars.

7

Turtlenecks make your bust look lower.

Who wants their breasts to look *lower*? The distance from the top of a turtleneck to the breasts is a long way down.

If you're wearing a turtleneck, make sure your bra is supportive and lifting, and add something over the turtleneck, like a V-neck or jacket.

8

Broad-shouldered women can wear halters.

Halter tops are a great way to show off shoulders. Because the lines of a halter make an "A" shape, it balances out the broad shoulders and the rest of the body.

Halter dresses with an A-line skirt are especially flattering on women whose shoulders are broader than their hips, because they add a little width to the bottom half.

9

Raglan sleeves will minimize broad shoulders.

Because raglan sleeves, which point in toward the neck, make an "A" shape, they minimize broad shoulders.

With no seam on the widest part of the shoulder, they leave a nice, smooth, rounded shoulder.

10

Narrow shoulders: How can we help?

You can make your narrow shoulders appear wider by wearing boat-neck or off-the-shoulder styles.

Puffy sleeves and shoulder pads also make narrow shoulders seem wider, and will balance out a wider bottom half if necessary.

11

You can enhance your upper body.

There are many tricks to help you look your best from the waist up.

If you know your proportions and how they balance each other, you can dress in a way that accentuates your best features, whether it is your chest, shoulders, neck or waist.

12

Show off your curved-in waist.

Even if you are blessed with an hourglass figure, you need to show it off so it looks its best. It is very important for you to wear clothing that keeps your waistline nipped in, otherwise it will look larger.

Belts at your natural waist, worn over looser tops or dresses will keep you looking like an hourglass.

13

Empire waist garments accentuate slim ribcages.

Empire waistlines on dresses or tops, which fit directly under the bust, accentuate the ribcage, which is usually the slimmest part of the body.

If a woman wants to hide a tummy, a top or dress that flows out from the empire waist is the perfect solution.

14

Vertical seams on jackets slim waist.

Structured jackets are well-known for slimming a shape and pulling together an outfit.

To give the illusion of a curved-in waist, look for curved or straight vertical seams in the front and/or back of a jacket.

15

Pockets on chest give larger appearance.

If you have a large chest, stay away from pockets in that area, especially detailed or bulky ones.

On the other hand, if you have a small chest, pockets can make it look larger and balance out the bottom half of your body.

16

Dark colors on top de-emphasize chest.

If you want to make your chest appear smaller, or take attention away from it, wear a darker color on top and a lighter color on the bottom.

To make a small chest larger, or large hips smaller, reverse the colors, with light color on top and a darker one on the bottom.

17

Wrap styles give everyone a waist.

Back to the hourglass figure: Wrap tops and dresses, made famous by designer Diane Von Furstenburg, will give you one. The wrap is one of the most flattering styles to come out in a long time.

A wrap dress or top will make you look feminine and curvy, no matter what your shape.

18

Avoid boxy shirt and jacket styles.

Why these were so popular in the 1980s and 1990s I don't know. They do not help anyone's shape.

Please take these shapes out of your closet and do not buy any more. Wearing a button-down shirt opened as a jacket has the same boxy effect.

Make Friends with your Bottom Half

19

Dark colors make bottom half smaller.

Okay, this is your chance to wear black. If you wear black trousers or skirt with a lighter top, depending on the shapes of each garment, your bottom half will appear smaller.

Because the black is not up against your face, the harshness of the color will not be an issue.

20

Cargo pants make thighs look larger.

Any pants or skirts with bulky pockets on the sides will make thighs and hips look larger.

This is great for someone with thin legs and a larger upper half or broad shoulders, because it will balance out her body.

21

Pants should be the perfect length.

Nothing ruins a look like jeans or trousers that are too short. They instantly look outdated, cheap, too small, or just old.

Standard pant length is one-half inch off the floor at the back of your foot, with shoes on.

22

Bulky jean pockets enlarge rear end.

It's easy to find jeans with all kinds of embellished back pockets, many with flaps that snap. These pockets can make your rear end appear larger, which is great if you have a small or flat rear end, but stick to flat, plain pockets if you want to minimize it.

23

Tapering causes ice cream cone effect.

Tapered pants and jeans were popular in the 1980s and 1990s. Like boxy tops, they never flattered anyone, and you should get rid of any old pairs you still have.

Because they taper down toward your ankles, which are already your narrowest area, they make everything above look bigger, like an ice cream cone.

24

Bleached and whiskered jeans enlarge thighs.

Manufacturers of jeans in Juniors departments are famous for putting fake wrinkles (whiskering) and bleaching right on the front of the thighs.

For young women with thin legs, it can be a great effect, but for women with more curvy thighs and hips, it looks out of place and will make thighs look larger.

25

Larger bottom halves love pencil skirts.

Not only are pencil skirts chic and sexy, they can make the hip area look smaller, especially if in a dark color and not too tight.

When worn with a lighter top, a dark pencil skirt will also help balance out narrow shoulders.

26

Make A-line skirts your best friends.

This is probably the most common skirt shape, for good reason. An A-line gives a feminine look to the body by providing movement, and hides stomach, hip and thigh flaws by floating away from the body.

It works well in many fabrics and prints, and goes well with jackets or simple tops.

27

Add needed volume with pleated skirts.

Yes, some women can use extra volume on the bottom. The extra fabric and fullness work well with a fitted top and give women with thin hips and thighs a nicely balanced body.

Some skirts that go with suits have pleats just around the bottom, which still look professional but add a little volume.

28

How to wear a ruffled skirt.

Ruffled or tiered skirts are both good choices if you are looking to add volume to your bottom half.

Wear them with fitted shapes on top, and keep the length right below the knee.

29

What is the right skirt length?

Currently, most fashion experts agree that the perfect skirt or dress length is right above the knee, right below the knee, or anywhere in-between.

More casual skirts can be shorter, especially on younger women and teens.

30

Can I still wear long skirts?

In general, long skirts, such as mid-calf to ankle, are not in style and tend to drag you down, especially for the workplace.

That said, ankle-length maxi dresses are making a comeback. So yes, you can wear long skirts, if they are new, in style and appropriate for the occasion.

To the Tips
of your Toes

31

Footwear can make or break you.

I read once that the first thing women notice about men is their shoes. If that's true, they probably notice other women's shoes even more.

Wearing the wrong shoes can ruin any attempt at a great outfit, while perfect shoes can make an average-dressed woman look and feel fantastic.

32

Ballet flats are the new heels.

Ballet flats--you have seen them everywhere. They have become a nice alternative for those who want to be more comfortable and do not like high heels.

They pair well with skinny jeans, wide pants and longer, fuller skirts, but tend to look dowdy with pencil skirts.

33

High heels will never go away.

While flats are a huge trend, high heels are very much alive and well, and flatter a woman's legs and entire shape.

Don't wear them with short shorts or skirts unless you're a 20-year-old runway model (or look like one), and make sure your pants are long enough to wear with them.

34

Bare legs are better than sheer.

By sheer I mean nude pantyhose that we all wore for years. This is a new fashion rule that I do not feel strongly about, but the new advice says that nude pantyhose should be avoided like the plague.

35

How to show off your legs.

If you follow the rule and do not wear nude stockings or pantyhose, but feel uncomfortable showing your bare legs, your options are tanning lotion, leg makeup, or solid or patterned opaque tights.

Pants are fine, but do not give up on more feminine, versatile skirts and dresses because of your legs.

36

Replace old pantyhose with new tights.

Tights are back in a big way, and there are hundreds of options to go with your dresses and skirts.

If you are more used to pantyhose, start choosing new skirts and dresses with tights in mind. Have fun with the many color and pattern combinations.

37

Square-toed chunky shoes are out.

This is probably the one item I have seen the most in women's closets. They were popular for a long time, especially in the 1990s, and were comfortable and versatile.

They are not in style anymore, and make any outfit look dated, and less feminine. They shorten the leg and look especially bad with skirts and dresses.

38

Shoes can be comfortable and cute.

Several comfort shoe brands are now making shoes that are fashionable as well as comfortable. Find them in department stores, specialty shoe stores, and online.

Regular brands can ease your pain as well, especially when supplemented with the right inserts. The important thing is to keep looking and don't give up. The right shoes for you are out there.

39

No dainty heels with cargo pants.

Make sure to match the proportion and style of your shoes to your pants or skirts.

An example I have seen is women wearing strappy, dainty heels with cargo capris. Cargo capris are very casual, almost hiker-looking, and should be worn with a more casual, flat, substantial shoe.

40

Don't wear athletic shoes with jeans.

This is one of the most disobeyed rules in the fashion world. We are talking about chunky, white shoes that are meant for working out in a gym, worn with any kind of jeans.

Better alternatives are non-athletic sneakers by makers such as Puma or Skechers. They look cute and stylish and are every bit as comfortable as gym shoes.

41

No white socks
with dark shoes.

Most people know this rule, but the sock issue for women wearing pants is a difficult one.

In cold weather, it just feels better to wear some type of socks, although it's not always the most fashionable look. As a rule of thumb, keep your shoes and socks close to the same shade, and keep socks neutral.

42

Ankle boots don't go with dresses.

There might be some disagreement on this, but in my opinion it just does not flatter a woman's legs or body.

Short boots are perfect for dress trousers and jeans when you do not need to wear knee-high boots. "Bootie" heels are the new exception, and go well with dresses and skirts.

Beyond Clothing: Finishing Touches are Vital

43

Keep updated on changing makeup trends.

Makeup is vitally important for bringing out your beauty. Watch for trends in the media. Right now, makeup is lighter both in color and thickness, which gives a fresher, more youthful look.

Take advantage of department store cosmetic counters for learning new color trends.

44

Get regular makeup advice from professionals.

Makeup advice could mean getting together once a year or season with a consultant who sells makeup and skincare from a company like Mary Kay or Arbonne International.

It's easy to get in a rut with makeup, so keep trying new things, and don't give up and go without makeup.

45

Good skin care can slow aging.

Taking care of your skin will slow the effects of aging. Good skin care includes twice-daily cleansing, toning and moisturizing, as well as regular exfoliating.

Sunscreen should be an everyday step, worn under makeup.

46

White teeth have become a necessity.

Have you noticed that everyone you see on TV or in a magazine has dazzling white teeth? This was not true ten or fifteen years ago. Just watch some old movies or TV shows.

Whitening strips are available at drug and grocery stores and work very well for the cost. They are easy and can be done at home. Having white teeth makes you look younger, happier and more put together.

47

Take care of fingers and toes.

Take a cue from Oprah Winfrey and others and consider keeping your nails shorter and more natural. Short nails are more "in" now, and they require less maintenance than longer artificial nails.

Nail colors come and go, and depend on your age, but clear or neutral polish always looks appropriate.

Any color is fine on toenails, just keep them polished.

48

Do you want to hold hands?

One of the most important pieces of beauty and anti-aging advice I would give young girls and women is to wear sunscreen on the tops of their hands.

Hands get extensive sun exposure, mostly from driving, and sunscreen used at an early age can prevent age spots.

If it's too late, try the many products or procedures available to help fade them.

Your Hair is your Crowning Glory

49

Visit your favorite hair stylist regularly.

Outdated or neglected hair can ruin the best makeup and clothing. Ask people whose hair you admire for the name of their hair stylists, and keep trying stylists until you find someone you like.

The important thing is to continue to get trims and any needed color, especially as you get older.

50

Watch magazine, movie and television trends.

Pay attention to characters' hairstyles in movies, television shows and news broadcasts.

Read magazines and look for styles that are popular and might suit you, then take a picture with you when you visit your stylist.

51

Washing your hair is not enough.

I have seen women out in public with wet hair. While all hair styles do not need to be blow-dried, leaving hair wet looks very unfinished.

Take a few extra minutes to blow dry, use the correct products, and style your hair.

52

How to understand overwhelming hair products.

Stylists agree that hair products do make a difference in the ability to control and style your hair.

Hair Stylists will tell you the most important products are good quality shampoo and conditioner, bought at a reputable beauty supplier or salon.

53

Blow dryers, flatirons and curling irons.

The quality of your flatiron is more important than the quality of your blow dryer. Use flatirons as little as possible and keep them away from your scalp. They can burn your hair at the scalp, and it will not grow back.

Refer to women's magazines or your stylist for tips on how to use styling tools.

What to do About the Weather

54

Finding the right outerwear is important.

Outerwear is easy to neglect in your wardrobe shopping. However, nothing ruins a beautiful formal or professional outfit like an old outdated coat, or a too-casual ski or rain jacket.

Remember to include outerwear in your clothing budget so you are not caught without a proper coat when you need it.

55

This office is absolutely freezing cold!

Why many offices and other buildings keep temperatures like a meat locker I will never know. Because I tend to be cold, I have found ways to keep warm without wearing an old cardigan all the time, such as layering clothing items, and wearing scarves and vests.

56

Keeping warm during the summer months.

This is not a problem in most parts of the country—unless you're in air conditioning all day, or live in Seattle or San Francisco, where it rarely gets truly hot, even in summer.

Think three layers—Layer 1: tank, camisole, or long-sleeved t-shirt; layer 2: top or blouse; layer 3: cardigan or jacket. Obviously the cardigan or jacket can come on or off, and layer 1 keeps layer 2 from not being enough.

57

Layering adds creativity, color and warmth.

Layering is a great way to mix colors and prints and show your creativity. Although it might seem like you need more items, it actually allows you to use those items more often because you are combining them in various ways.

For climates that tend to get chilly, even indoors, learning how to layer can keep you warm *and* stylish.

58

Use scarves to their full advantage.

The scarf, worn around the neck in every conceivable configuration, has gone from a plain woolen necessity for freezing weather to a fashion accessory worn even in the summer.

So take advantage of the trend and collect scarves in various prints and colors. They make a big difference in your warmth, and will add color and interest to your outfits.

59

What did we do without vests?

Down or "puffy" vests have been around for awhile now, but have expanded into different designs, fits and fabrics, to work with a variety of casual outfits

Vests can be the top layer of an outfit that can be taken on or off as the temperature changes. Add a coordinating scarf and it is easy to go without an extra jacket.

60

Rain, rain, go away. Not happening!

I live in the Seattle area, and rain is a part of life that I have to consider when deciding what to wear.

In Seattle, I have found that a more dressy, parka-style waterproof coat with a hood works for all but the dressiest occasions. When more dressed up, you should wear a trench or wool coat without a hood and use an umbrella.

61

Are you feeling hot, hot, hot?

Enough about keeping warm, what about keeping cool in the summer?

While attending my daughter's college orientation in Tucson, Arizona, I found that cotton sleeveless dresses were cool, comfortable, and looked perfectly appropriate around the other parents and University personnel.

62

Avoid the trap of spaghetti straps.

While spaghetti strap garments will definitely keep you cool, they are a bad idea for women with large chests and better suited to younger girls and beach or pool settings.

Sleeveless tops and dresses are just as cool, and much more polished and professional for most women.

63

Don't be afraid of flip flops.

Keeping your feet out of closed shoes makes a big difference in keeping cool.

Fortunately, there are hundreds of styles of fairly dressy sandals and even flip flops that work for all but the most conservative or dressy settings.

Learn to Shop Without the Drop

64

Shop for your best colors first.

When shopping, first determine your best and worst colors from a color expert, or by draping yourself with various colors in a mirror.

Once you know your colors, make that your first priority when scanning the clothing racks. It narrows the field down quite a bit.

65

Get to know your sales staff.

Sales staff at better department stores know their merchandise, know fashion and can be a great help to you. If you can get to know specific sales people and their work schedules, that is even better.

Take advantage of their expertise and think of every shopping trip as an education and an opportunity for new ideas, not always resulting in a purchase.

66

Be realistic about your spending limits.

I am very guilty of not following this rule. I love to look at designer handbags and shoes that I will never buy.

This is fine to get an idea of what is new and to refine your taste, but can be a big time-waster that keeps you from finding appropriate items for your wardrobe that fit your budget.

67

What fun is a clothing budget?

Setting a budget for clothing can be fun when you feel good about yourself for saving money and sticking to your budget.

Even if you do not always stay within budget, it is a good method for keeping track of what you spend on clothes so that when you need to set a realistic budget, you'll be ready.

68

Don't be taken in by outlets.

Outlet malls can be fun, but be careful of buying things you do not really need because of the assumption that everything is a bargain.

I have noticed that most outlet mall prices are about the same as sale prices at regular stores, which are frequent. You probably will not get ripped off at an outlet store, but make sure you only buy items you love.

69

Shop only for your body shape.

A wardrobe consultant or stylist can take your measurements and determine your body type.

Once you know your body's shape and proportions, your shopping trips will be more focused because you will be looking only for clothing styles that flatter your unique body shape.

70

Explore all of your shopping options.

Take advantage of the alternatives to traditional mall and department store shopping.

Along with online shopping, pre-shopping on the internet can enhance your trip to the mall. Browse online at items at your favorite stores before you go to see what might be on sale, and what is new and available.

71

How to use a personal shopper.

Personal shoppers can be employed by department stores, which obviously only shop in that particular store.

A wardrobe or image consultant will have already sorted through your existing wardrobe and know your best colors and clothing shapes, making the process easy for you. She can help you shop at a variety of stores, rather than representing one store.

72

Mix high end with low end.

It is O.K. to wear inexpensive items of clothing or accessories with very expensive ones.

If you like to splurge once in awhile on a designer item, or find it on sale, do not be afraid to mix it with something from an inexpensive store like Old Navy.

Mixing up your shopping habits will help to mix up your wardrobe, which is a good thing.

It's Off to Work you Go

73

Why look your best at work?

You are the face (and body) of your company. How do you want to portray your company and the services you provide? What message are you sending?

Impressions (not just first) do count. Yes, people should get to know the real you, but they will not always be given that opportunity. Why make it difficult for people to have a good impression of you?

74

Messy clothing looks like messy worker.

If your clothing is not well put-together, it might appear that your work-life and/or company is disorganized as well.

There is a reason the whole "Dress for Success" movement has been at the forefront for so long—there is some truth to the saying.

75

Business suits can be separates too.

This idea is not brand-new, but is makes so much fashion sense. Buy a matched business suit, including jacket with pants, skirt or both.

Then look for ways to wear the separate pieces with other items, like a sweater with the pants, the jacket with dressy trouser jeans, or a more textured jacket with the pants. Multiply your outfits!

76

Softer clothes can be professional, too.

If you do not feel that structured jackets fit your fashion style or personality, you can find alternatives that are still appropriate in the corporate workplace.

There are a multitude of sweater styles now that are softer in appearance and feel, but still work with a professional outfit.

77

Dress a dress up or down.

Dresses are easy. Easy to put on in the morning, easy to look coordinated. Keep several dresses in your wardrobe that can be paired with a jacket for a professional work look, or with a shawl and fancier shoes for a dressier look.

78

Casual Friday: What do I wear?

Casual Fridays in many companies have become casual every day, which to some people means, "wear whatever you want," or "dress like you are at home."

While you probably will not get fired for dressing as if you are at home, why not give yourself an edge in your career and make a better impression?

79

All jeans are not created equal.

In the last decade or so, jeans have completely evolved from something you wore camping or to the grocery store to a mega fashion statement with prices to match.

They are now more comfortable, much more flattering, come in styles that are acceptable for evenings out, and are perfect for casual work settings.

80

Wear the *right* jeans to work.

Basically, most jeans older than ten years should not be worn in a casual workplace, or at all for that matter. (Save them for camping).

Wear newer jeans to casual workplaces with nice t-shirts, sweaters, layered looks, cardigans and jackets. They truly go with anything on top.

81

A word about dressing work-appropriate.

The biggest mistakes people make in dressing for work are dressing too young, or too provocatively.

Outfits that show too much skin, or reveal too much because of being too tight, are completely inappropriate for any work environment and don't flatter women at all.

Dress Her Up, Take Her Out

82

Plan in advance for special events.

A formal evening or big event takes detailed planning, so do not wait until the last minute to think about what you are wearing. It will save you money, too.

For winter and holiday season parties, start in October to look for the clothing and accessories you will need. Better yet, shop after the holidays for next year.

83

Show off your very best asset.

While looking for a special dress for a special occasion, choose one or two of your best body areas to show off some skin.

If you have toned arms and shoulders, buy something sleeveless. If you have great legs, wear something short. The idea is to focus on one area instead of showing everything.

84

Save some money for special bling.

Once you have found the dress or outfit, the process has just begun. Again, planning ahead will allow you to find the perfect jewelry pieces to complete your outfit.

New, stylish costume jewelry that goes with your dress is more modern than tiny, dated fine jewelry.

85

The finishing touches: the perfect accessories.

Of course, you do not want to ruin your beautiful new evening dress and jewels with a too-casual coat, boring shoes, or your everyday handbag.

If you shop for accessories throughout the year, you can usually find pieces that will go with most evening dresses; they do not need to be perfectly matched.

86

Complement, don't match, shoes and bags.

Your evening bag should not match your dress or shoes, but complement or "go." Any kind of neutral satin or metallic will go with a colored dress, or use a jewel-toned bag with a black dress.

It's also better if shoes and bags do not match each other, but coordinate with all the items in your outfit. Beware of sparkles on too many items.

87

Wraps, coats and jackets and furs.

Cropped jackets made of brocade, velvet or fur are good choices for evening. There are also many types of wraps and shawls to choose from, in cashmere, wool and other fabrics, which work well with evening dresses.

If you must really bundle up, wear a basic black wool coat and use the coat check when you arrive, if possible.

88

Accessories add pattern, texture and shine.

Accessories are just as important to your everyday look as they are for a special occasion. They add the same thing to your overall look that they do to your home—the pizzazz that complements your clothing.

Look for various patterns, textures and types of shine in your accessories to coordinate with your clothing.

89

Never too many shoes or bags.

While possessing a large number of shoes and bags is not as necessary as having enough clothing, if you can afford them and enjoy them, they are the best ways to add variety and interest to your outfits.

So you can never have too many, as long as you're using them in creative ways to enhance your clothing.

90

Shop for accessories all year long.

Sometimes you need something specific to go with a special occasion outfit, as discussed in the previous chapter.

However, I find that it works just as well to shop for accessories whenever you are out. Were you invited to a home jewelry party? Just buy something you like that suits your style, and it will likely go with something you own.

Everyone Has Her Own Special Style

91

How to determine your unique style.

There are many books and magazine articles that categorize a woman's style or fashion personality.

Once you find your personal style, you can be consistent with what you wear, will find shopping easier, and will be more content and comfortable with how you look. You will truly be yourself, and always look your best.

92

What are the fashion style categories?

If you work with a style, wardrobe or image consultant, part of the process will be answering questions about your lifestyle, habits, and preferences, in clothing and other parts of your life.

This will determine whether your style is conservative, chic, urban, bohemian, edgy, artsy, whimsical, or a combination of styles.

93

Your style depends on your age.

As you get older, you can still express your style, but be careful about going to the extreme, and dressing too young.

Your personal style, whether bohemian or dramatic, needs to be expressed appropriately as you age. Watch the Juniors departments for trends, but shop for different versions of those trends, which will usually be more subtle and of better quality.

94

Who wants to look too old?

Well of course no woman over, say, 35, wants to look older than she is. However, women make themselves look older all the time.

Wearing old, out-of-date clothes is probably the most aging habit I see. Also, clothing that is too long and baggy drags you down and ages you. Other aging habits: matchy-match outfits, harsh or no makeup, and gray hair.

95

Undergarments are part of your style.

Shapewear has become quite a phenomenon in the last several years. There are now hundreds of choices for smooth, comfortable, supportive garments that truly make a difference in how your clothes look and fit.

Undergarments in the bike short style are high-waisted and slim any bulges around your waist, hips and thighs.

96

The right bra makes the difference.

I know, this is not a fun thing to talk about or shop for, but it is an often neglected garment. The right bra makes your clothes look better, and makes you look taller, leaner and younger.

A saggy chest makes you look both older and heavier, and could be easily lifted a few inches with the right bra.

Good department store personnel are trained to help, so take the plunge!

97

You deserve to be beautiful underneath.

While shaping undergarments are fairly plain, and have a place in your lingerie drawer, make room for some undergarments that make you feel pretty, even if nobody sees them.

There are enough choices out there that have enough support for most days, but show some beauty and style as well.

98

Give your closet its due respect.

Your closet and drawers should be treated like the vital tools that they are in your ongoing determination to look your best.

If your clothing is not organized and visible in a closet, it keeps you living in the past, makes it difficult to create new, flattering outfits, and wastes your valuable time.

99

Keep your closet in good shape.

Organizing your closet is the first step in your new goal to look your best.

Evaluate each item, using what you learned from this book to determine whether or not you should keep it.

Put remaining items back in your closet and drawers with similar items. Hang up as much as possible, but do not hang outfits together. Use shelves to keep folded items visible.

100

Transform yourself from the outside in.

By following the lessons in this book, whether on your own, with a wardrobe consultant, style coach, friend or family member, you will feel more confident and positive about yourself.

Confidence leads to success in anything you choose to do to share yourself with this world and make a difference. You will be transformed from the outside in.

See the entire Six~Word Lesson Series
at *6wordlessons.com*

Want more great Wardrobe advice?
Check out
wardrobe~consulting.com

Read more about the author at
pattypacelli.com